Spotlight on Social Justice

USED OR ABUSED?

ADVOCATING FOR ANIMAL RIGHTS

ALEXIS BURLING

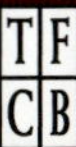

TWENTY-FIRST CENTURY BOOKS / MINNEAPOLIS

For Mark, Suki, LB, and all the rest of the deer, bears, sheep, cougars, and other animals that wander onto our property.

Twenty-First Century Books™
An imprint of Lerner Publishing Group, Inc.
241 First Avenue North
Minneapolis, MN 55401 USA

For reading levels and more information, look up this title at www.lernerbooks.com.

Main body text set in Bembo Std Regular
Typeface provided by Monotype Typography.

Library of Congress Cataloging-in-Publication Data

Names: Burling, Alexis, author.
Title: Used or abused? : Advocating for animal rights / Alexis Burling.
Description: Minneapolis : Twenty-First Century Books, [2026] | Series: Spotlight on social justice | Includes bibliographical references and index. | Audience term: Children | Audience: Ages 11–18 | Audience: Grades 7–9 | Summary: "From research to entertainment to food, people rely on animals for many purposes. But what are the potential consequences of that? And what's being done to lessen them? Dive into the history and present of animal rights in North America"— Provided by publisher.
Identifiers: LCCN 2024038756 (print) | LCCN 2024038757 (ebook) | ISBN 9798765644133 (library binding) | ISBN 9798765684931 (paperback) | ISBN 9798765683033 (epub)
Subjects: LCSH: Animal rights—History—Juvenile literature. | Animal welfare—History—Juvenile literature.
Classification: LCC HV4705 .B87 2026 (print) | LCC HV4705 (ebook) | DDC 179/.309—dc23/eng/20241227

LC record available at https://lccn.loc.gov/2024038756
LC ebook record available at https://lccn.loc.gov/2024038757

Manufactured in the United States of America
1 – CG – 7/15/25

CONTENTS

INTRODUCTION

When we think about animals, some might immediately envision wild creatures such as wolves and bears that forage for food to survive. Those who work on farms might imagine the horses that help herd sheep or the pigs that make up a portion of the world's food supply. Others might picture the critters we keep as pets and consider them part of our families.

For thousands of years, animals have been appreciated and utilized for various purposes. But they've also been maltreated or exploited. Some animals are taken from their natural habitats to be used in biomedical research. Doctors use monkeys to study life-threatening human diseases such as cancer and multiple sclerosis. Scientists experiment with rats in cosmetic labs to determine the safety of makeup products. Other animals are bred for food or entertainment. Some farmers and slaughterhouse workers corral cows and chickens into cramped, unsanitary spaces before they slaughter the animals and sell them for consumption. Poachers kill elephants for their valuable ivory tusks. Organizers of illegal fighting rings raise roosters and bully breed dogs such as American pit bull terriers and American Staffordshire terriers to compete to the death.

Advocates for animal rights emphasize that animals should be treated with kindness and respect. This includes not harming them or using them in ways that cause them pain. Animal rights supporters also want stronger laws to protect animals and encourage finding better ways to care for them.

This book will explore how animals have been poked, prodded, and abused for the benefit of humans. It will also highlight some of the national and international laws surrounding animal rights and organizations fighting to prevent the mistreatment of animals.

CHAPTER ONE

Medical and Cosmetics Testing

Medical testing on animals involves giving them specific medications or treatments to see how they react. This helps scientists determine if these medications or treatments are safe and effective for humans. Medical research on animals includes studying animals to understand diseases, genetics, and biology. This can help scientists treat human illnesses and learn more about how living things work. Cosmetics testing on animals checks whether beauty products, such as makeup and shampoo, are safe for people to use.

All these tests and research help make sure products, medicines, and treatments are safe for humans. For example, researchers made many medical breakthroughs by first testing medications or surgical procedures on animals to assess their efficacy. Polio—a disease that killed millions of people globally in the twentieth century—was almost completely eradicated thanks to a vaccine that researchers first tested on animals to ensure its safety. Similarly, researchers have removed harmful ingredients from products such as hair dye and eye makeup after discovering their toxicity during tests on animals. In 1933 an untested chemical called p-phenylenediamine in mascara blinded more than a dozen people in the US and caused the death of one. This ushered in an era of animal testing required by the US Food and Drug Administration (FDA) to verify the safety of cosmetics before use.

Proponents of animal testing in medical research and cosmetics testing argue that using animals provides insights that are often directly applicable to human health. Animal testing enables scientists to study diseases, develop treatments for those diseases, and produce safe medications or products. Opponents of the practice say medical and cosmetic testing on animals is inhumane because it inflicts unnecessary pain on helpless subjects who can't consent. Anti-testing advocates insist other viable methods exist to reach the same goal.

A Debate throughout History

The arguments for and against animal testing in medical and cosmetic research are complicated. As far back as the 300s BCE, Greek scientists such as Aristotle dissected animals in anatomical studies to better understand the human body. These surgeries, called vivisections, were performed on live animals to learn how sensory and motor nerves worked in the body. Throughout the Age of Enlightenment (1685–1815), an intellectual and cultural movement that prioritized reason over superstition and scientific proof over religious faith, the practice continued. French physician-physiologist François Magendie, a pioneer of experimental physiology who practiced in the nineteenth century, attempted to learn how facial muscles worked by dissecting a dog's face while its paws were nailed down.

In the 1870s people all over England—including Queen Victoria—spoke out against what they considered to be a cruel practice. In 1875 the Victoria Street Society for the

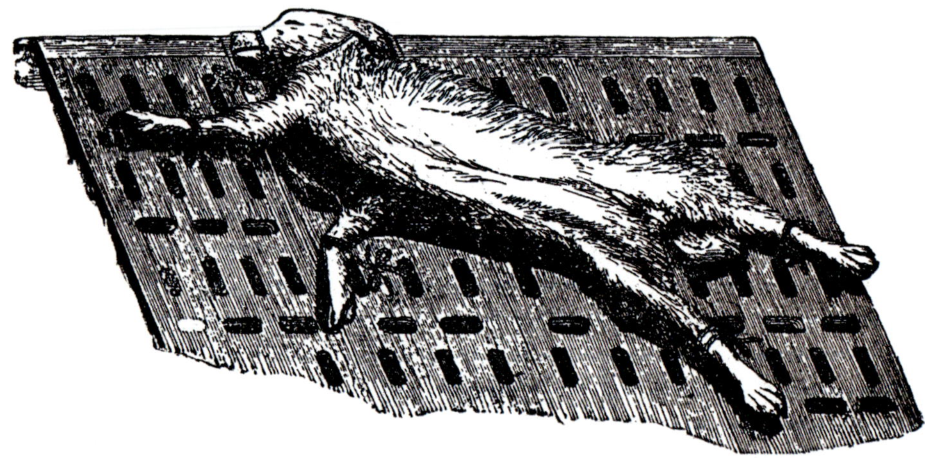

During the Age of Enlightenment, French philosopher René Descartes and his followers believed that animals were unthinking machines without the ability to feel pain. This belief justified performing experiments on live animals without moral concerns.

Protection of Animals Liable to Vivisection was founded. It was the first internationally recognized society for animal protection in the medical field.

In 1937 more than one hundred people in fifteen states died after ingesting elixir sulfanilamide, an untested medication that turned out to be poisonous. This tragedy led to the passing of the Federal Food, Drug, and Cosmetic Act of 1938. This law gave the FDA the authority to regulate the safety of food, drugs, medical devices, and cosmetics, often through animal testing.

By the mid-1900s the attitude toward animal testing for medical and cosmetics research shifted. Though scientists and lawmakers still believed in the value of the practice, many argued there should be more protections for lab animals. In 1965 New York Representative Joseph Resnick introduced the Laboratory Animal Welfare Bill in Congress. This led to the passing of the Animal Welfare Act (AWA) in 1966.

Historians consider the AWA to be an early milestone of the animal rights and anti–animal-testing movement. Among other protections, it mandates that all animals intended for use in research facilities, including dogs, cats, nonhuman primates, guinea pigs, hamsters, and rabbits, must be given humane care and treatment. The AWA is still the primary federal law in the United States regulating the treatment of animals. Since its passage, it has been amended several times to improve the standards of care and expand the range of animals covered.

Cures and Vaccines

Medical facilities worldwide still use animals to conduct biomedical research. Experts in favor of the practice argue that animals are biologically similar to humans and can provide important answers to medical questions without jeopardizing people's health. For example, scientists frequently use mice in lab research experiments because they share more than 98 percent of their DNA with humans.

Many research programs justify performing experimental surgeries or testing drugs on animals because they are susceptible to many of the same health problems as humans, such as heart disease, cancer, diabetes, and asthma. Most animals also live shorter lives than humans, meaning a disease or experimental treatment can easily be studied throughout an animal's lifespan and across several generations. In addition, animal testing can reveal dangerous or life-threatening side effects of medications or treatments, such as congenital disabilities in offspring, infertility, or liver damage. And US federal law mandates that animal research must happen before research on humans to show the safety and efficacy of new surgeries or treatments.

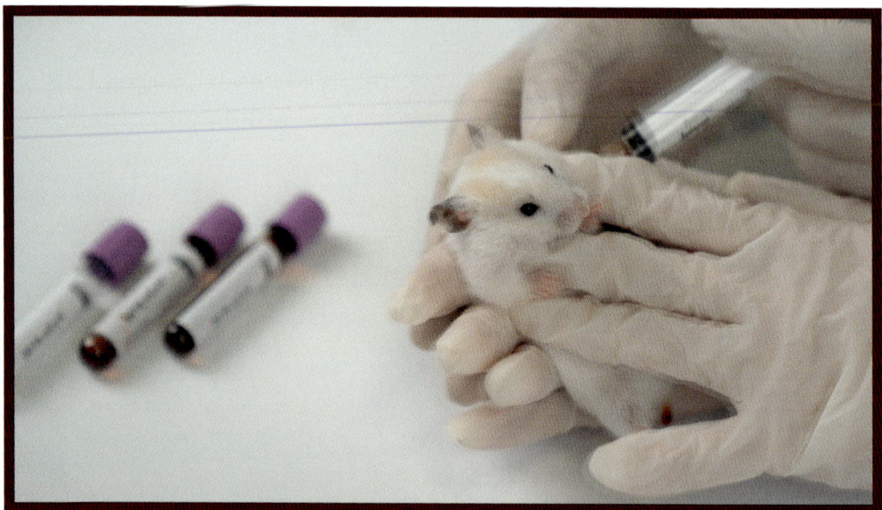

Scientists continue to test the safety and effectiveness of COVID-19 vaccines on animals. Scientists often use hamsters because they can easily be infected by the COVID-19 virus and their illness is similar to that of humans. Scientists use these hamsters to test if vaccines can prevent the virus from causing illness and study how the immune system responds after vaccination.

Many people think medical testing on animals is cruel. But proponents argue that many medical breakthroughs would have been impossible without animal testing. These breakthroughs include modern anesthesia; vaccines for life-altering or life-threatening illnesses, such as tuberculosis, human papillomavirus virus, and COVID-19; treatment for lethal diseases, such as acquired immunodeficiency syndrome, smallpox, and breast cancer; and lifesaving or prolonging surgeries, such as hip replacements, kidney transplants, and blood transfusions.

Because of modern advancements in technology and scientific innovations, there are now more alternatives to using animals in clinical and biomedical research. Researchers can use small 3D chips made from human cells or tissues donated by human volunteers to study everything from skin allergies to the development of new medications. Scientists can use computer models of the heart, lungs, kidneys, skin, or digestive systems to conduct virtual experiments. Physicians increasingly rely on clinical trials with willing participants, such as those suffering from fatal diseases, to determine the effectiveness of new medications.

Cosmetics Testing

Unlike medical testing on animals, which many scientists see as a necessity, some scientists consider cosmetic testing to be avoidable and cruel. Cosmetics testing occurs when cosmetic companies use animals—mostly rabbits, mice, rats, and guinea pigs—to determine whether products such as makeup, skin creams, hair products, and fragrances are safe for human use. Without administering any pain relief, researchers drip the products into animals' eyes, dab products onto their shaved skin, and even force-feed products to them to see if there's an adverse reaction. At the end of tests, animals are killed by asphyxiation, neck-breaking, or decapitation to prevent further suffering.

In the US, the FDA does not require cosmetic products to be tested on animals before they are sold. But cosmetic companies are encouraged to use testing methods to ensure product safety. Some companies still use animal testing even though it is not always reliable. For example, skin allergy tests on guinea pigs only predict allergic reactions in humans 72 percent of the time. According to the

REFLECT

The US has no federal laws that ban cosmetics testing on animals. Why do you think that is? Do you think cosmetics testing is worse than medical testing, or should both be allowed or banned? Why?

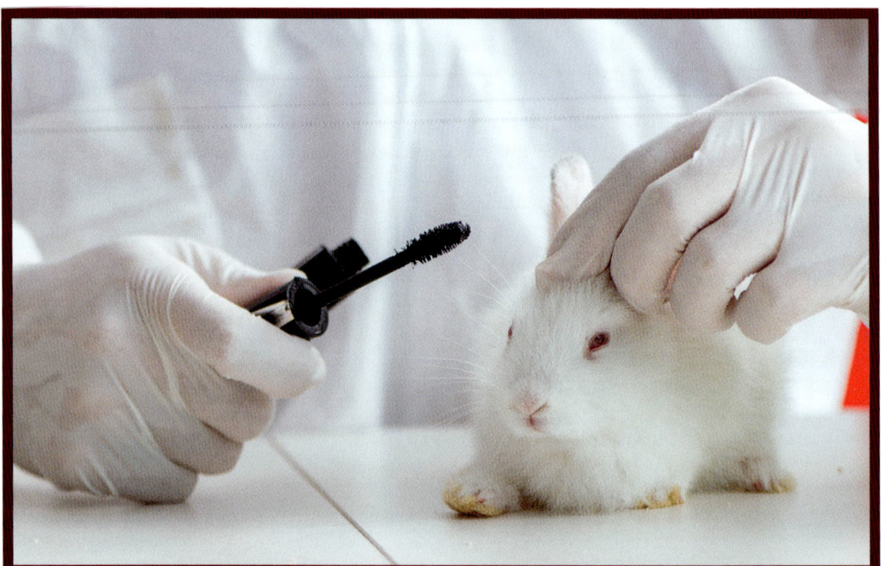

Eye irritant tests on rabbits only predict human reactions 60 percent of the time. This means that the results from these tests might not be reliable in determining a product's safety for people.

Humane Society, five hundred thousand animals worldwide die in cosmetics tests every year.

What's Being Done

Animal welfare organizations, activists, and concerned citizens raise awareness about the suffering of animals used in cosmetics testing. In the late 2010s AnimaNaturalis Mexico and the Animal Alliance of Canada organized protests and petition drives, calling to end animal testing in the cosmetics industry. In 2020 AnimaNaturalis and Humane Society International conducted public awareness campaigns using social media and held visually impactful demonstrations which created a groundswell of public support. In response to this public pressure, the Mexican government banned cosmetics testing on animals in 2021. Canada banned it in 2023.

New advancements in technology mean that scientists can test cosmetic ingredients with human cells or computer-generated models instead of on animals. As a result, many cosmetics companies are stopping animal testing. Forty-five countries, including Australia, Brazil, and South Korea, now prohibit cosmetics testing on animals. Though the US has yet to ban the practice, more than three hundred cosmetics companies support the Humane Cosmetics Act. It was introduced to the US Congress in September 2023 and would ban cosmetics testing on animals. Several states, including California and New York, have also banned the sale of cosmetics tested on animals.

As of 2024 the debate over animals being used in medical research and testing continues. In January 2024 the Environmental Protection Agency (EPA) decided not to move forward with a plan to stop using animals for medical testing by 2035. Some experts felt that new methods, such as computer simulations or testing cells in petri dishes, weren't advanced enough to fully replace animal testing. They argued that these new methods couldn't mimic the complicated ways a real living

In 2011 AnimaNaturalis activists wore rabbit masks as they protested animal testing for cosmetic products in Mexico City. The sign reads, "How many animals has your cream killed?"

body works. They thought more time was needed to improve these new methods before animal testing could be completely stopped. "We need to focus on what the science is telling us in order to advance methods that don't involve animal testing," says Chris Frey, the EPA's assistant administrator for research and development. "Fully phasing out animal testing is the goal, and we will always have that goal. But I don't want to get ahead of our scientists."

Despite this setback, several US organizations are educating the public about the downsides of using animal testing in biomedical research. The Physicians Committee for Responsible Medicine works to end animal testing by promoting alternative methods such as human tissue analysis and computer modeling. The Johns Hopkins Center for Alternatives to Animal Testing helps scientists find better ways to research medicines and diseases without using as many animals. They work with government agencies, pharmaceutical companies, and medical universities to create new methods that reduce animal suffering, use fewer animal subjects, and even avoid animal testing altogether.

Computer modeling is a promising alternative to animal testing. Researchers have developed models that predict whether a drug will cause heart arrhythmias more accurately than animal testing.

Canadian, US, and Mexican humane societies advocate for reducing and eliminating animal

Cruelty-Free Apps

Many consumers who care about animal rights wish to use products that aren't tested on animals. Several websites and apps track which products are or aren't cruelty free. The Leaping Bunny app is available for free. It alphabetically lists more than two hundred US and Canadian companies certified cruelty-free under the Leaping Bunny program, which ensures that all participating companies have not used animal testing during product development. Users can also scan an item's barcode to immediately determine whether it has been tested on animals. Two other similar apps are Bunny Free by People for the Ethical Treatment of Animals (PETA) and Cruelty Cutter.

More than two thousand companies have joined the Leaping Bunny Program, including Dr. Bronner's, eos, Method, YesTo, and Seventh Generation.

testing. They work on legislative campaigns and public education to promote humane and effective alternatives to the practice. The National Anti-Vivisection Society (NAVS) works to stop animal testing by pushing for new laws that protect animals and funding scientists who develop new, humane testing methods. NAVS also trains companies to adopt cruelty-free testing methods and improve their practices.

CHAPTER TWO
Animals as Food

How our food is sourced—especially meat, dairy, eggs, and seafood—is another hot-button animal rights issue. According to the GRACE Communications Foundation, a nonprofit organization dedicated to research and education on food production practices, "the modern, industrialized way in which we produce meat, eggs, and other animal products has turned animals into units of production, subject to inhumane treatment, terrible living conditions, and cruel deaths. In this system, to maximize efficiency and profits, companies and operators of concentrated animal feeding operations prioritize rapid growth and large-scale production over animal health and welfare."

Groundbreaking Reporting

In 1964 English activist Ruth Harrison published *Animal Machines*, a book that uncovered inhumane and unhygienic practices in the United Kingdom's livestock and poultry processing industry. As a result of both the public uproar and another series of opinion pieces and anti–factory-farming articles, the UK Farm Animal Welfare Committee created the Five Freedoms of Animal Welfare in 1965. These guidelines stated that any animal had the right to be able to stand up, lie down, groom themselves, and be free of distress or discomfort, thirst or hunger, and pain or disease throughout their lifetime, even if they were bound for the slaughterhouse. Since the creation of the Five Freedoms of Animal Welfare, farmers, ranchers, and other food production workers have adapted and used the guidelines to create animal welfare protocols and regulate how animals are raised for food.

Industrialized Production

In some ways, not much has changed in large-scale industrial farming since the publication of *Animal Machines*. Even though some people now run smaller farms where cows, pigs, and other animals can roam freely, animal rights activists say that many problems still exist in raising animals for food. More than 60 percent of the world's eggs—from nearly 4.5 billion hens—are still produced in industrialized factories as of 2024. Hens are packed into crowded warehouses, often in wire cages barely large enough for the birds to turn around in. These cages prevent the birds from spreading their wings and engaging in natural behaviors such as pecking or preening. This lack of movement can lead to broken bones, bloody feet, and emotional problems, such as hens attacking each other or pecking out their feathers.

Pigs raised for pork are often weaned from their mothers too early and jammed into small pens with other piglets. Some factory farms clip the piglets' pointed teeth to prevent them from injuring other piglets. Dairy cows are tethered by chains around their necks in small cages called tie stalls and artificially impregnated yearly so they can produce six

Notice that the pigs in this photo have no tails. Many farmers cut off pigs' tails, called docking, without anesthesia to prevent tail biting. Tail biting occurs in the stressful and overcrowded conditions of factory farms. Tail biting can lead to infection so docking is used as a preventative measure despite the pain it causes the animals.

to ten times as much milk as a cow naturally would. Many adult dairy cows suffer from mastitis—the inflammation of breast tissue—because they are milked by udder-clamping machines numerous times a day. The truck journey from farm to factory is also filled with noise, pollution, and terror for animals. The animals do not receive food, water, or protection from the weather on the way to the slaughterhouse.

What's Being Done

Some farmers are working to keep the animals they raise for food healthy and safe while they're alive. Will Harris, a fourth-generation farmer and cattle rancher in Bluffton, Georgia, transformed his 5,000-acre (2,023-ha) farm from one that relied on industrialized meat production to one that used a more humane model. Instead of keeping his animals in cramped, crowded pens for most of the day, Harris raises ten livestock species on open pastures, allowing the animals to graze freely and express their natural behaviors until their death. Harris's farm, White Oak Pastures, is also one of the only farms in the US to operate two on-farm slaughterhouses for processing red meat and poultry. This spares the animals the potential fear and harm of transport and ensures a humane end of life.

REFLECT

Making specific dietary and clothing choices is one way consumers weigh in on animal rights issues. Do you think one person's choices about what they buy or what they wear can make a difference in the lives of animals? Why or why not?

Switching to a humane farming model might initially cost more due to investments in better living conditions for animals and setting up slaughterhouses on-site. But over time, it can save money by reducing the need for veterinary care and medications. "I act as caretaker, creating conditions for my animals that are close to what nature would provide if I was not there at all," Harris says. "It's pretty simple: cows were born to roam and graze; chickens were born to scratch and peck; hogs were born to wallow and root. Deny them that right, and you have poor animal welfare."

Other farms such as Zeal Creamery in Missouri and Working Cows Dairy in Alabama are working with certified humane and animal welfare approved certification programs that ban tie stalls for dairy cows, mandate access to the outdoors for all farm animals, and offer guidance on how farmers can reduce cows' stress and pain from milking. States including California, Colorado, Florida, and Michigan have

Pasture-raised chickens get to roam around and eat a natural diet of bugs, plants, and seeds. Their eggs have twice as much vitamin E, beta-carotene, and omega-3 fatty acids compared to eggs from non-pasture-raised chickens.

passed laws to phase out the use of gestation crates—tiny cages where pregnant pigs are confined during pregnancy—in pork production. Hundreds of companies have enacted policies to raise 100 percent of their egg-laying hens without cages and sell only cage-free eggs by 2025, including Whole Foods, Costco, Wegmans, and WinCo Foods.

Many individuals are taking action too. While it hasn't directly impacted the prevalence of traditional industrialized farming methods, an increasing number of consumers choose to shop more responsibly by buying cage-free eggs and meat, poultry, and dairy products that have the "certified humane" or "animal welfare approved" label on the packaging. Others have adopted an animal cruelty–free diet to object to the way animals are bred and raised for food. As of 2024, 4 percent of Americans, 7.6 percent of Canadians, and 19 percent of Mexicans are vegetarians. These are people who don't eat meat or seafood for moral, religious, or health reasons. Some people also choose a lifestyle called veganism. They don't eat or use any products from animals, including clothing. About 2 percent of Americans, 5 percent of Canadians, and 9 percent of Mexicans are vegan.

What about Leather?

Shoes are often made of animal-derived materials such as leather or suede. Leather and suede come from the hide or skin of an animal—mostly cows, but also goats, pigs, and sheep. This leather is often a by-product of the meat industry. In other instances, however, animals are killed just for their skins. In China, the world's leading exporter of leather, an estimated two million dogs and cats are killed every year to make shoes, bags, and jackets for consumers. Other animals that are killed for their skins include alligators, lizards, ostriches, snakes, and zebras.

Some companies use mushrooms to make a cruelty-free leather alternative. Mushroom leather is soft, lightweight, waterproof, breathable, and completely biodegradable.

CHAPTER THREE

The Trouble with Trophy Hunting

In North America and around the world, many people hunt animals for food or clothing. They follow what many hunters consider to be an agreed upon code of ethics. They obey hunting, safety, and endangered species protection laws and pay attention to licensing requirements. They only hunt where permitted and avoid trespassing on private property. They make sure to aim carefully to kill the animal quickly. And they use as much of the animal as possible before discarding any waste.

But another practice has long been considered controversial not just by animal rights activists but also by some hunters. Trophy hunting is tracking and killing an animal for entertainment. Some people do it for the thrill. Others trophy hunt to hang an animal head on their wall or display a hide on their floor for decoration. For example, former US president Theodore Roosevelt was an avid trophy hunter. He and his son killed more than five hundred animals in just one African safari trip in 1909. Trophy hunters such as Roosevelt pay large sums of money—anywhere from $10,000 to more than $70,000 depending on the type of animal hunted and the length and location of the trip—to travel around the world and kill animals for entertainment.

Record High Figures

The US is the world's largest importer of hunting trophies, which include the entire dead animal or just part of the animal such as the skull, teeth, or skin. According to the US Fish and Wildlife Service, between 2016 and 2020, more than seven hundred thousand wildlife trophies were imported to the US. The so-called African Big Five animals—prized because of their reputation for being the hardest and most dangerous to hunt on foot—are lions, elephants, African rhinos, leopards, and African buffalo. Hunters also seek other animals such as American black bears, Hartmann's mountain zebras, and gray wolves. Sixty-eight percent of animals hunted for trophies are shot and killed in Canada, with other populations coming from South Africa, Namibia, Mexico, Zimbabwe, New Zealand, Tanzania, Argentina, and Zambia. More than one hundred thousand threatened or endangered animals are killed for trophies every year.

In the US, wildlife-killing contests—events in which participants win prizes for killing the most or largest bobcats, coyotes, foxes, mountain lions, or other animals within a specific time period—are legal in forty states. More than six hundred contests take place every year. Thirty-three states allow the trophy hunting of black bears, including females with cubs, which increases cubs' mortality rates.

The problem is also widespread in Canada and Mexico. Between 2012 and 2022 trophy hunters in British Columbia, Canada, shot more than 40,500 black bears, 2,200 cougars, and 8,500 wolves. The trophy-hunting industry in Mexico is

Between 2010 and 2021 trophy hunters killed nearly half a million black bears in the US. In some states, such as Maine and Wisconsin, hunters kill more than four thousand black bears annually.

valued at approximately $200 million. There are nearly four thousand trophy-hunting companies or ranches in Mexico.

Canned Hunts

From small exotic-animal safaris to large groups such as the US-based Safari Club, organizations around the world run trophy-hunting expeditions. Some even specialize in canned hunts, events that feature animals bred in small enclosures, raised in captivity specifically for the sport, and trained to become accustomed to human contact so they're easier to kill.

Representatives from these organizations say that the money raised from trophy hunting goes towards conservation efforts in surrounding communities. But experts argue this is often not the case. In some areas, such as South Africa, the hunting operators or local government officials often keep the money for themselves. That is one of many reasons—in addition to animal cruelty—why animal rights activists argue trophy hunting should be strictly regulated or entirely stopped.

Threatened Species

Trophy hunting can decimate animal populations, some of which—such as the southern white rhino and the African leopard—are already threatened or on the verge of extinction. Trophy hunting targets animals with special features such as giant horns or sharp tusks. This hunting can make these animals go extinct faster. For example, trophy hunters often prefer to shoot the largest and strongest animals, typically males. Once these animals are killed, their strong genes are often lost to future generations, and the animals' absence in general threatens those left behind. Killing the strongest male lion in a pack leaves the remaining adults and cubs vulnerable to competing prides. A new dominant lion will always try to kill a rival's cubs in a hostile takeover. The strongest male in a pride also keeps younger males in check, so eliminating it might cause less-experienced, aggressive adolescent lions to spread out into surrounding human communities, attacking people and eating their livestock. Trophy hunting has contributed to a nearly 50 percent decline in wild African lion populations over the past three decades.

REFLECT

Why do you think some people believe trophy hunting is acceptable while others oppose it?

What's Being Done

Some countries and regions have made efforts to ban trophy hunting and trophy imports. Kenya, once a top destination for international hunters, banned trophy hunting in 1977. They did so because of declining wildlife populations, habitat destruction, and corruption within the trophy-hunting industry. Other countries followed suit, including Malawi,

Costa Rica, India, and Colombia. Finland, France, the Netherlands, and Belgium have banned the import of hunting trophies from endangered species.

In the United States, efforts to end trophy hunting and importing have been less successful. In 2019 the Conserving Ecosystems by Ceasing the Importation of Large Animal Trophies (CECIL) Act was proposed. This law was named after a lion named Cecil who was illegally killed by a trophy hunter. The CECIL Act aimed to ban the import and export of animal trophies listed as threatened or endangered under the Endangered Species Act, a law passed in 1973 that protects these animals and their habitats. The CECIL Act also would have stopped the US Fish and Wildlife Service from dispensing import permits for trophies from African lions or elephants hunted in Tanzania, Zimbabwe, or Zambia. Although the US House of Representatives approved the CECIL Act in 2019, the US Senate did not, disappointing many animal rights activists.

Despite the setback of not passing the CECIL Act, dozens of international organizations are working to stop trophy hunting and address the related decimation of animal populations and their habitats. Elephant Aid International, Wildlife SOS, Wild Aid, and Pro Wildlife are some of the groups tackling the problem. In July 2022, 136 conservation and animal-protection groups from around the world got together to push policymakers to ban trophy imports.

In 2016 protesters in London joined the Global March for Lions, calling for an end to the hunting of captive lions bred for trophy hunters in Southern Africa.

"In the face of the [human-made] global biodiversity crisis, it is unacceptable that exploitation of wildlife simply for acquiring a hunting trophy is still permitted and that trophies can still be legally imported. It is high time that governments end this detrimental practice," says Dr. Mona Schweizer of Pro Wildlife.

A Lion Loved by Many

On July 1, 2015, dentist Walter Palmer from Minnesota did something many people worldwide considered unforgivable. He paid $54,000 to bow hunt a black-maned, thirteen-year-old lion named Cecil who lived in Zimbabwe's Hwange National Park. Cecil was beloved by tourists and locals. His death sparked international outrage, with people using social media to condemn trophy hunting altogether. Two years later, Cecil's son Xanda was also killed in a trophy-hunting incident.

In response to Cecil's death, the United States, the largest importer of lion trophies, added new protections for lions under the Endangered Species Act in 2016. More than forty-two airlines—including Delta, American Airlines, and Air Canada—initiated bans on transporting trophies of Africa's Big Five. As of 2021 Cecil's former pride has expanded. Now led by brothers Humba and Netsai, Cecil's pride consists of twenty-five lions, including Cecil's mates, offspring, and grandcubs.

Cecil the lion (*pictured*) was comfortable around vehicles, so people could see him up close, and he was known for his shaggy black mane.

CHAPTER FOUR

Problems with Poaching

Illegal poaching threatens the existence of animals such as elephants, tigers, and rhinoceroses. Wildlife poaching is when hunters illegally traffic or kill certain animals and sell parts of their bodies. Thousands of animals are kidnapped from their natural habitats and trafficked every year.

Globally, poaching is estimated to be worth between $70 billion and $213 billion every year. China is the biggest importer of illegal wildlife, with the US coming in close second. Many consumers buy and sell these animals as exotic pets or covet their byproducts. For example, in 1986 the International Whaling Commission banned hunting whales for profit. This rule made hunting whales illegal in most countries but it allows limited, regulated whale hunts for Indigenous communities who rely on whaling for cultural purposes.

Killing for Resources

Big game and other, smaller animals are illegally poached for many reasons. In Africa and Asia, the highest-value targets for illegal poachers are elephants and rhinoceroses. Since 2008 poaching gangs have killed approximately eleven thousand rhinos in Africa for their valuable horns. Rhino horns are made of keratin, an ingredient frequently used in Chinese medicine and in Vietnam for its alleged cancer-curing properties. Between 2014 and 2017 poachers illegally killed at least one hundred thousand African forest elephants for their tusks. The tusks were sawed off and sold to make luxury products such as statues, art carvings, and jewelry. Poachers usually shoot elephants and rhinos with guns or tranquilizing darts, remove their horns or tusks with chainsaws, and leave them to die.

Poachers also hunt animals in parts of Mexico to sell mainly to Chinese markets. These include turtles for pets and

Members of the Kenya Wildlife Services mobile veterinary unit sedate and treat a wounded giraffe. The giraffe had a poacher's snare caught on its leg. Giraffes are poached for their pelts, bones, hair, and tails. People make jewelry out of giraffe hair and their tails are highly valued in some cultures.

meat, and crocodiles for skins to be made into footwear and clothing. Along the Mexican border with Belize and Guatemala, poachers kill jaguars primarily for their paws and teeth, which are ground up and used in Chinese medicine. Rare birds, such as macaws, are captured and sold as exotic pets.

In Japan, Norway, and Iceland, poachers have killed nearly forty thousand whales for their meat and body parts since the commercial whaling ban took effect in 1986. More than one hundred thousand dolphins, small whales, and porpoises are killed in other countries every year. Their oil, blubber, and cartilage are used in pharmaceuticals and health supplements.

Long-Lasting Impacts

As with trophy hunting, poaching has a disastrous effect on wildlife and the people who live around the poached species. Extinction of such species is the greatest threat. Experts say the sub-Saharan black rhinoceros is at risk of extinction because of extensive poaching. As of 2024 only six thousand members of the species remained, compared to one hundred thousand less than fifty years ago.

Every case of poaching can trigger biodiversity loss. Once one animal's population declines, it has a ripple effect down the food chain that is hard to recover from. Hunting and killing predators means there are fewer of them to keep prey populations in check. Biodiversity loss can also permanently alter the physical environment. For example, a decrease in the number of elephants—large herbivores that help shape the landscape by knocking down trees and stomping down brush—can lead to overgrowth of certain plant species. This alters the habitat and can make it unsuitable for other animals native to the region.

Saving the Vaquita Porpoise

The vaquita porpoise is the world's most endangered marine mammal. It only lives in Mexico's Upper Gulf of California. In 2021 scientists estimated that only ten of these sea creatures remained. Vaquitas are nearly extinct because poachers target the endangered totoaba fish. The fish live in the same area as the vaquitas. Poachers sell the totoaba's swim bladder for thousands of dollars for use in traditional medicine. Poachers use illegal gillnets—very long nets that trap not only totoabas but also vaquitas, dolphins, whales, and sea turtles. Since 2015 the Sea Shepherd Conservation Society has helped the Mexican government remove more than one thousand gillnets from the Upper Gulf of California. By removing these gillnets, they have saved more than four thousand animals, including some vaquitas.

Little is known about vaquita porpoises. The closest sighting of a vaquita has been from 300 feet (91 m) away.

Rampant poaching can also have a devastating effect on the livelihoods of local people. In regions that depend on wildlife viewing for tourism, safety concerns and the threat of poaching can negatively impact the economy. If tourists stop visiting an area for fear of encountering poachers, the area will make less money. But protecting animals from poaching is a dangerous task. For example, the ivory trade in Africa is linked to corrupt and violent armed militia groups who will stop at nothing to get their prize. In the Democratic Republic of the Congo's Virunga National Park, at least 170 park rangers were murdered by gang leaders running poaching operations between 1999 and 2019.

What's Being Done

The United Nations' Convention on International Trade in Endangered Species of Wild Fauna and Flora regulates the wildlife trade. This group formed in 1973 and consists of 184 member countries. It monitors more than forty thousand targeted animal and plant species worldwide to help ensure their protection.

Save the Rhino is an international organization dedicated to protecting rhinos, reducing illegal rhino trade, engaging local communities in threatened areas, and educating the public about what they can do to help stop rhino poaching. Save the Elephants was formed in 1993 to advocate for anti-poaching laws, fund local education initiatives, and research elephants in their natural habitat. In partnership with the Wildlife Conservation Network, it runs the Elephant Crisis Fund, which works to dismantle the world's ivory trade.

In the United States and Mexico, several national groups are working on the front lines to stop poachers. These include the World Wildlife Fund, Snow Leopard Trust, and International Anti-Poaching Foundation. The US government also set aside approximately $116 million in 2020 to increase anti-poaching efforts worldwide by strengthening law enforcement teams, investigating and prosecuting wildlife-trafficking crimes, and forming new partnerships with international anti-poaching groups in countries such as Mexico, South Africa, China, Peru, and Thailand. In November 2020 secretary of state Mike Pompeo approved

In 2016 a member of the Save the Elephants team watched over the elephants at Samburu National Reserve in Kenya. The Samburu region has the second-largest group of elephants in Kenya. Elephant defenders have watched over this group of elephants day and night for more than twenty-five years to protect them from poachers.

a new visa-restriction policy targeting people believed to be involved in wildlife trafficking. These US government efforts have led to some successful enforcement actions but the need for community involvement remains critical to improve these anti-poaching efforts.

Many US states have bans on owning exotic animals too. As of 2024 twenty-one states have bans on all exotic pets considered dangerous, such as wild cats, large non-domesticated carnivores, reptiles, and nonhuman primates. Four states don't have any laws related to exotic-animal pet ownership, including Alabama, Nevada, North Carolina, and Wisconsin.

CHAPTER FIVE

Pet Stores and Pet Mills

Whether it's ethical to own pets has stirred up debate for ages. Is it morally right or healthy to keep a Great Dane inside a cramped urban apartment? Should a cockatoo that mates for life and can live from forty to sixty years in the wild be relegated to living alone in a cage inside a person's house? For many animal activists, pet ownership has inherent problems, including a lack of outdoor access, reduced exercise, an unnatural diet, and a high potential for neglect. "Because they are bred to be dependent on us, the basic relationship between humans and companion animals is flawed because of the difference in power," says Doris Lin, a director for the Animal Protection League of New Jersey. "This relationship forces animals to love their owners to get affection and food, often neglecting their animal nature to do so."

Despite these ethical concerns, there's nothing more heartwarming for many people than adopting a new pet. Many people believe that having a pet can be beneficial for the animal. Pets living with humans have a safe and secure home, protecting them from predators and harsh weather. Pet owners provide toys, exercise, and activities that keep pets mentally and physically stimulated, preventing boredom. Pets often live longer than their wild counterparts due to the veterinary care, balanced nutrition, enrichment, and protection they receive from their owners. But there are risks involved in choosing pets, especially when dealing with breeders or pet stores.

Are All Breeders Bad?

As of 2024 around 66 percent of US households own at least one pet. In Mexico, about 70 percent of people do. In Canada, that number is almost 80 percent. More than half of these homes consider their pets members of their family. But across North America, there are also millions of stray animals roaming the streets, many of whom remain outdoors their entire lives or wind up in shelters. More than seven million animals in the US end up in shelters each year. While no-kill shelters exist, many overpopulated kill shelters euthanize old, sick, or unpopular animals to make room. Of the nearly three million cats and dogs euthanized in shelters annually, approximately 80 percent are healthy and could have been adopted.

Despite the high shelter populations, most estimates show that only 23 percent

Bengal cats are popular purebred pets. They can cost anywhere from $500 to $4,000.

of Americans adopt dogs from shelters. Why? Part of the reason is that many people prefer purchasing their pets from a breeder. Animal breeders are people who selectively breed animals with specific traits and sell the offspring for profit. Some breeders breed hybrid or "designer" breeds, which mix different breeds for specific traits. Other breeders raise purebred animals.

Many dogs, such as pugs, are bred for their appearance rather than their health. Pugs are susceptible to breathing complications, skin infections, chronic pain, and more.

There are many arguments for and against buying a pet from a breeder. Some reputable breeders are certified by official programs such as the American Kennel Club's Breeder of Merit Program or the Cat Fancier's Association. These breeders use a breeder code of ethics to ensure the animals they raise and sell are kept in clean, bright, and warm places, with regular vet checkups and plenty of care and food. But breeding animals just for specific physical traits can cause health problems and make the animals suffer. Exaggerated features developed through breeding can cause physical and emotional health issues. Selective inbreeding, especially in dogs, can lead to blood disorders, metabolic issues, and weaker immune systems.

The Truth about Pet Mills

Pet mills are commercial facilities with factory-like conditions that specifically breed animals—usually dogs and cats—in large numbers for sale through pet stores or directly to consumers through classified ads or the Internet. According to PAWS, an organization dedicated to sheltering or adopting out stray cats and dogs, about 90 percent of puppies sold in pet stores nationwide are from these mills. But pet stores don't check on the breeding conditions—and many prospective owners don't know enough about the topic to research it.

REFLECT

What are some reasons a potential pet owner might want to adopt a pet from a breeder? Are these reasons ethical? Why or why not?

In many cases, animals raised in pet mills are kept in small cages in overcrowded spaces, without any room for exercise. Sometimes the animals aren't properly protected from extreme heat or cold, receive no medical attention, or don't receive enough socialization and affection. As a result, the animals can experience infections, malnutrition, physical abnormalities such as swollen or bleeding paws, or severe tooth decay. Some female animals are kept at pet mills for the entirety of their lives just to give birth to offspring. When they can no longer do so, many are sent to kill shelters or abandoned.

There are more than ten thousand puppy mills in the United States. The US Department of Agriculture regulates fewer than three thousand of them. What's more, the AWA—the only federal law that regulates the treatment of animals in research, testing, transportation, and exhibition—doesn't make a clear distinction between animals from pet mills and those from farms. This lack of oversight means the animals raised in pet mills often don't get the protection they need. There are sixteen states in the US that don't have humane pet sale laws that prevent pet stores from selling puppies and kittens from pet mills, including Arizona, Missouri, North Carolina, and Vermont.

What's Being Done

Much of the unethical breeding and selling of pets is hard to detect because many of these breeders operate in secret. They may use private homes or hidden facilities, making it difficult for authorities or animal welfare organizations to find them. Some places don't have strict laws to control these unethical breeding practices. Uninformed consumers unintentionally support these breeders when they purchase pets from them. Groups such as the American Society for the Prevention of Cruelty to Animals (ASPCA) are actively working to inform people about pet mills and irresponsible breeders.

Humane Canada is a group with more than 7,500 members. It works with 121 animal shelters across the country to end commercial dog mistreatment through rescue and adoption programs. Another group, Animal Justice, lobbies the Canadian government to dismantle pet mills and prevent the abuse and neglect of pets in homes. In Nebraska, Hearts United for Animals operates a no-kill animal rescue and sanctuary that's dedicated to rehabilitating animals who have suffered from mistreatment or abandonment. It has rescued more than twelve thousand dogs from pet mills and provided low-cost spay or neuter services to more than fourteen thousand animals. This helps keep stray and shelter animal populations low.

Around 2.6 million puppies originating from puppy mills are sold annually in the US.

The ASPCA's Criteria for Responsible Breeding

The ASPCA recommends that all people looking to adopt a pet first consider animals from shelters or rescue groups. They require that breeders must do the following to be ethically responsible:

- Give animals quality food, clean water, proper shelter, exercise, socialization, and professional veterinary care.
- Keep animals clean and well-groomed.
- Prioritize health and function over appearance when breeding and screen for heritable traits that could negatively impact offspring.
- Provide potential adopters with accurate and reliable health, vaccination, and pedigree information.
- Create an adoption contract that includes the breeder's responsibilities, adopter's responsibilities, health guarantees, and return policy.

In 2017 California became the first US state to prohibit pet stores from selling animals from pet mills. In 2022 New York Governor Kathy Hochul signed the Puppy Mill Pipeline Act into law, making New York the fifth US state to ban the sale of puppies, kittens, and rabbits in retail pet stores.

There are also organizations targeting pet ownership. The Pet Advocacy Network is made up of veterinarians, retailers, groomers, pet food suppliers, and individuals from around the world who are working to educate the public about being a responsible pet owner. They advocate for fair animal care standards, promote the physical and emotional benefits of the human-pet bond, and represent the pet care community on product safety issues.

CHAPTER SIX

Using Animals for Sport

Every year since 1875, more than 150 thousand people gather on the first Saturday of May in Louisville, Kentucky. They gather at Churchill Downs, a horse-racing complex, to see which three-year-old thoroughbred horse will beat the rest of the nineteen. The rider of the fastest horse takes home a $3 million prize.

Many consider the Kentucky Derby to be one of the most exciting and glamorous sporting events. But as with many sports involving the use of animals—including greyhound racing, sled dog racing, rodeos, and fights involving animals such as roosters or dogs—there are downsides for the animal participants. Animal rights activists argue that when animals are used in sports, they are often mistreated, and their welfare isn't properly considered. The right thing to do, they insist, is to ban the practice altogether.

Horse Racing

Horse racing has roots in the earliest Olympic Games in ancient Greece, around 700 BCE. With renowned horse racing events, including the Kentucky Derby, Preakness Stakes, and Belmont Stakes, the modern practice is a $25 billion business in the US and an $8.7 billion business in Canada.

But while the sport might be a fun annual tradition for people, it's often a death trap for the horses involved. Since 2014 ten thousand racehorses have died during their racing tenures. Recent findings by the Horseracing Wrongs organization suggest that more than two thousand horses die at US tracks every year. They mostly die from heart failure or bleeding in the lungs from overexerting themselves, either during the race or after the race has finished. Other fatal injuries include broken necks, severed spines, ruptured ligaments, and shattered legs. The thousands of horses who age out of the sport or can't perform well are often killed or butchered.

Training is also hard on racehorses. Foals are taken from their mothers at six months old and tamed by age two so they become submissive and compliant. They're kept in 12-by-12-foot (3.66-by-3.66-m) stalls for more than twenty-three hours a day and are only let out for training. Some trainers scream at them, yank their reins, or strike them with a whip to get them to go faster. The horses are considered property that's bought and sold.

Thoroughbred racehorses can run at speeds of up to 40 mph (64 kmh), making them some of the fastest land animals in the world.

But there are some laws that protect racehorses. In 2020 the Horseracing Integrity and Safety Act established standards for racetrack safety, medication control, and anti-doping measures. Many states have their own regulations concerning the treatment of racehorses. These can include standards for housing, feeding, veterinary care, and conditions of racetracks.

Fighting Competitions

Unlike the controlled environment of the racetrack, where horses compete based on their speed and agility, animal fights involve brutal and illegal contests. From roosters to pit bulls, countless animals are made to competitively fight one another. An estimated forty thousand people in the United States are involved in professional dogfighting, a sport illegal in all fifty states. Why? Winning dogs can earn their owners as much as $100,000 per fight.

Dogs in fighting competitions are often bred specifically for the sport and raised in isolation. Owners often keep them chained up in cramped cages and give them performance-enhancing drugs such as anabolic steroids to enhance muscle mass and encourage aggression. Owners

Dogfighters may crop a dog's ears to prevent injuries to the ears during fights or to make the dog look more aggressive. The procedure can be painful for the dog.

make the dogs fight repeatedly until the dogs either die during competition or are killed inhumanely afterward. The owners most often kill them by electrocution, drowning, hanging, burning, or shooting. Dogfighting owners will often kidnap untrained, weaker dogs as bait dogs—dogs meant for competitors to practice their fighting skills on.

REFLECT

Do you think the government should enact and enforce stricter laws that prevent animal fighting? Why or why not? What are some ways that they might do that?

Cockfights are also vicious. Breeders raise millions of birds on US farms for the sport. Many birds are chained to a stake in a dark box and injected with steroids and adrenaline-boosting drugs. Some birds are trafficked to places where the sport is popular, including Mexico or the Philippines. Gambling on birds generates billions of dollars a year in revenue. In cockfights, the birds are forced to fight to the death. Most have knives or icepicks called gaffs attached to their legs to make the fights bloodier.

What's Being Done

In Mexico, there are cockfight bans in the states of Sonora, Coahuila, Quintana Roo, and Veracruz. But cockfighting remains an issue in some areas due to cultural traditions and inadequate enforcement of laws. Dogfighting and cockfighting are both illegal in Canada. Canadians charged in connection to dogfighting rings receive a prison term of up to five years or a fine of $10,000. Several US laws protect animals from fighting ventures too. Cockfighting is a crime in all fifty states. In forty-three states, it's illegal to be a spectator at fights. In thirty-nine states, raising or selling

How the Internet Changed Fighting Competitions

In the days before the Internet, people would have to hear about a dogfight or cockfight through word of mouth and then drive to a secret location to watch the fight live. But with the advent of social media, a fight can take place and be viewed anytime. In 2017 one Facebook user in Virginia posted a play-by-play of a nearly two-hour dogfight while thousands of followers watched. In 2018 a Michigan-based dogfighter used WhatsApp to share gruesome videos of animals fighting. The Internet also gives owners easier access to dogfight training information. A few online searches can tell a dog owner how to use a slat mill—a treadmill made for dogs—to condition their animal. Videos can show a dogfighter how to use a flirt pole—a stick with a bungee cord—to improve an animal's endurance. Those interested in breeding fighting dogs can also learn about bloodlines from online forums.

birds for fighting is illegal. And in twenty-nine states, it's illegal to own animal-fighting gear.

The AWA bans animal fighting, including breeding animals for fighting and attending animal fights. Lawmakers have updated it many times to strengthen penalties and address emerging issues in animal-fighting practices such as online platforms and illegal gambling. Dogfighting has been a felony under federal law since 2007, with maximum penalties of a $250,000 fine and three-year imprisonment. In 2023 two US representatives introduced the Fighting Inhumane Gambling and High-Risk Trafficking Act to Congress, which would strengthen protections for at-risk birds and dogs.

Farm sanctuaries rescue roosters from cockfighting and provide them with medical treatment for their injuries. These sanctuaries create a safe and calm environment where the roosters can recover and live peacefully, free from the violence of their pasts.

"Every day, countless animals endure horrific violence as people force them to fight for personal gain," said Representative Andrea Salinas of Oregon, who helped introduce the act. "Cockfighting, dogfighting, and other blood sports are inhumane and unsafe—and Congress must intervene to protect innocent animals from such abuse."

Still, dogfights and cockfights keep happening. The Anti-DogFighting Campaign is an international organization that educates the public about dogfighting abuses and advocates ending the sport worldwide. They collaborate with local law enforcement and animal control officers to crack down on suspected breeding dens and animal-fighting gambling rings. Last Chance for Animals advocates for abused horses, dogs, roosters, and other animals used in sports. The organization also runs a Don't Be Cruel campaign in schools to teach young people about animal fighting competitions. The Stand Up for Pits Foundation in Los Angeles, California, has operated a tip line for illegal dogfights since 2015. It also runs dog adoption programs and advocates for greater protection for pit bulls and other bully breeds, which are frequently used in fighting competitions.

CHAPTER SEVEN

Animals as Entertainers

Animals have long been used to entertain humans, from zoos and aquatic theme parks to cameos in movies and television shows. Proponents of the practice insist the animals aren't harmed during the process and are cared for. But opponents argue that places such as circuses and stages are terrible environments for animals because they can inflict irreversible physical, psychological, and emotional damage, sometimes even leading to death.

Marine Mammal Parks

Some marine mammal parks and aquariums allow the public to observe aquatic species and learn about the diversity of marine life. The Monterey Bay Aquarium in Monterey, California, is a world-renowned research facility with large tanks for the animals. Scientists and other staff study marine species, their habits, and the detrimental impacts of human activities on their ecosystems.

But other types of marine mammal parks are less humane. Some feature bottlenose dolphins, sea lions, or orca whales that perform tricks in front of a cheering audience. Training

The 2013 documentary *Blackfish* drew the public's attention to the suffering of orcas at parks such as SeaWorld. Director Gabriela Cowperthwaite believes the film helped inspire orca protection laws in California and Canada.

for these stunts can be harmful to the animals. Sometimes trainers withhold food or incentivize orcas and dolphins with excessive treats as motivation to get them to perform tricks. This can cause weight loss or gain and aggressive behavior. Too little weight can make orcas and dolphins physically weak, while excess weight leads to joint and mobility issues.

Living in small aquariums are also contrary to the animals' natural behaviors such as hunting and migration. Orcas and dolphins are complex beings that live in tight-knit groups in the wild. Whales travel around 100 miles (161 km) in a single day. When housed in a small, artificial aquarium—sometimes as tiny as 24 by 24 feet (7.3 by 7.3 m) and 6 feet (1.8 m) deep—these sea creatures are deprived of their natural social connections. They must swim endlessly in circles, which leads to physical and emotional distress, behavioral abnormalities, and a shortened lifespan. In the wild, dolphins use echolocation to navigate and locate their prey by bouncing sonar waves off surrounding objects. In cramped tanks, these waves bounce off the walls, causing dolphins immense distress and confusion.

Other physical injuries from living in tight tanks include dorsal fin collapse, eye irritation and skin peeling from the chlorinated water, and infections due to germs from constant contact with humans. In the wild, dolphins live between twenty and forty years, male orcas live between thirty and sixty years, and female orcas live between fifty and ninety years. But captive orcas typically die within the first ten years of captivity, usually before they reach the age of twenty-one. Most dolphins die within the first two years of captivity.

Zoos

Like many marine mammal parks, zoos are places where formerly wild animals are kept in cages or enclosures for public display. Zoos such as the Toronto Zoo in Canada or the Chapultepec Zoo in Mexico help deepen visitors' understanding of the natural world. They teach about habitat conservation, biodiversity protection, and efforts to combat poaching and trophy hunting. Some zoos also help reintroduce endangered species back into the wild. In 1985 there were only nine California condors left in the state. In 1987 the San Diego Zoo and the Los Angeles Zoo created the California Condor Recovery Program to breed and reintroduce California condors to the wild. The birds were bred and raised at the zoos. As of 2024 more than 560 California condors exist, with more than 280 of them living in the wild.

P.T. Barnum's Scandalous Sideshow

One of the earliest instances of keeping whales in captivity occurred more than one hundred years ago. In 1861 circus tycoon P.T. Barnum paid for the capture of two beluga whales near L'Isle-aux-Coudres (Elbow Island) in Quebec's St. Lawrence River. He planned to put the whales in a 40-by-18-foot (12-by-5.5-m) brick and cement tank in the American Museum in New York City. The whales were transported by train in boxes filled with barely enough water to reach their blowholes. Two days after arriving at the museum, the whales died. Still, Barnum considered the exhibit a success. He advertised their quick deaths in captivity to get more people to come to the museum. Over the next four years, nine more whales were captured and displayed at Barnum's sideshow. Most died soon after their transfers. In 1865 the last two belugas died when the entire museum burned down in a fire.

In the wild, beluga whales swim about 70 miles (113 km) per day. They can live up to 70 years. The are very social animals and communicate through facial expressions, physical contact, whistles, and clicks.

Bears are highly intelligent animals and travel 20 to 40 miles (32 to 64 km) each day in the wild, using their keen senses to find food and explore new territories. In captivity, their natural behaviors are often restricted, leading to physical and mental suffering.

But despite these benefits, zoos are seen by some as places where animals are kept in crowded enclosures against their will and to the detriment of their health. Many animals don't have enough space to practice their normal behaviors, especially larger animals such as apes, tigers, polar bears, and cheetahs. This can lead to obsessive behavior such as pacing, as well as diseases associated with being in captivity. About 70 percent of adult male gorillas in North America suffer from heart disease, the leading cause of death among gorillas in captivity.

As with marine mammal parks, zoos can be psychologically damaging to their residents. Researchers who study zoo animals often find they suffer from problems not seen in the wild, such as anxiety in giraffes, depression in leopards and gibbons, and obsessive-compulsive disorder in brown bears. Many animal behavior experts attribute these psychological disorders to the animals' confined environments; the introduction of stimuli, such as camera flashes, that aren't found in the wild; and a lack of socialization opportunities with other animals in their species. Animals may also face boredom and frustration due to the absence of natural foraging opportunities and exploration.

Animal Actors

From Lassie the dog to Flipper the dolphin, animal actors have been stars on the stage and screen. From the 1870s to the 1920s, bears, monkeys, elephants, and dogs were featured in theatrical variety performances called vaudeville shows. Performers trained the animals to do various tricks and stunts, which delighted audiences.

Though animal performances in movies and television remain common and beloved, many people question whether the practice is ethical. Animal trainers claim they do everything possible to ensure animals aren't mistreated while the

Jimmy the crow was born in captivity near sea level in California. In 1951 Jimmy collapsed due to the high altitude in Utah, where he was performing on location for the movie *The Lion and the Horse*. His trainer, Curley Twiford (*pictured*) got a portable oxygen tank and tent to help him get better.

camera is rolling. But many animal rights organizations argue when animals act in movies and television shows, it goes against their natural instincts. Additionally, many animals are injured or die during productions. This is due to demanding filming schedules, unpredictable weather, or unforeseeable accidents.

What's Being Done

In 2019 Canada passed a landmark bill banning the captivity of whales, dolphins, and porpoises, with violations punishable by fines of up to 200,000 Canadian dollars. No US federal laws prohibit the display of orcas in captivity. In fact, the Marine Mammal Protection Act specifically permits the capture of wild orcas for education and entertainment. But public outcry over reports of an orca breeding program and rampant dolphin abuse at SeaWorld Orlando in 2016, as well as a slew of deaths at Miami Seaquarium between March 2019 and April 2020, has brought more attention to the issue.

Similarly, the laws surrounding zoos and zoo animals are minimal. In Canada and Mexico, there aren't any federal laws that specifically protect zoo animals. Though some zoo animals in the United States fall under the protections of the AWA, the law excludes protection for birds and cold-blooded animals such as reptiles, amphibians, and fish. Despite the lack of guidelines, there are some organizations and activist groups working to fight for more protections on the state and local levels. The American Zoo and Aquarium Association is made up of representatives from more than 235 zoos in the United States and abroad. It dedicates millions of dollars every year to support scientific research, conservation, and education programs. It also creates guidelines around veterinary care

In the US, more than 183 million people visit zoos that are accredited by the American Zoo and Aquarium Association each year. This number is higher than the total yearly attendance for all major professional sports—basketball, football, hockey, and baseball—combined!

and nutrition, global species population management, and animal welfare in accredited zoos and aquariums.

There aren't any existing laws in the United States that protect animal actors. But in 1988 the American Humane Association created the Guidelines for the Safe Use of Animals in Filmed Media as part of the Humane Hollywood Initiative to help ensure animals are properly protected. These standards require filmmakers to provide proper housing, food, and veterinary care for any animal that appears in a film. To get a No Animals Were Harmed certification to appear in the credits, any movie or documentary must have an animal safety representative present during filming to monitor and report any violations.

CONCLUSION

Animals Need Our Help

From medical testing to factory farming to trophy hunting to poaching, there are many longstanding animal rights issues that lawmakers and the public throughout the world face. Many experts say that humans have already accomplished a lot when it comes to protecting animals and their welfare in medicine, sports, and entertainment. But animal rights activists argue we still have a long way to go. For many people on the front lines of animal rights issues, the end goal is to put a stop to or severely limit all human activities that cause animal suffering in any way or form. This includes industrial farming practices, animal experimentation in scientific research, zoos and animal theme parks, pet mills, and more.

The good news is there's a lot that people can do to fight for animal rights. As the animal rights organization Humane Decisions puts it: "Animals need our help—whether they are farm animals, animals in your backyard, wild animals whose habitat is endangered, domestic pets, animals used for entertainment, or abandoned and homeless animals." Even the smallest step forward makes a difference.

Promoting Animal Rights in Your Community

You can play a significant role in promoting animal rights and supporting animal welfare within your community. Here are some ways you can get involved:

- Volunteer with your local animal shelter or rescue organizations to help care for animals and assist with events such as dog walk fundraisers.
- Write letters to local government officials advocating for stronger animal protection laws.
- Support animal rights causes by signing and sharing petitions.
- Start or join a community or school club focused on animal rights and welfare.
- Share your knowledge about animal rights with your friends and family. Create posters, flyers, or social media posts to educate friends and family about the importance of animal rights.

By standing up for animal rights, you can help create a world where every creature is treated with kindness and respect. Your voice matters—take action for those who can't speak for themselves and make a lasting impact!

GLOSSARY

activist: someone who actively campaigns for social or political change, often by participating in protests, demonstrations, or other forms of direct action

advocate: to publicly support or recommend a particular cause, policy, or idea. An advocate is one who supports or promotes the interests of a cause or group.

anabolic steroid: a drug that mimics the effects of testosterone, promoting muscle growth and strength. It is often misused and can cause serious health issues in humans and animals.

anesthesia: a procedure used to prevent patients from feeling pain during surgeries or medical treatments

asphyxiation: the state of being deprived of oxygen, usually by strangling or suffocation, which can result in loss of consciousness or death

biodiversity: the variety of all living things in a particular area

concentrated animal feeding operation: a large-scale agricultural facility where many animals are crammed into a small, tightly populated space for feeding

ecosystem: a connected group of plants and animals and their physical environment

efficacy: how well something works or achieves its intended purpose

ethical: relating to moral principles and the discussion of whether something is right or wrong

euthanize: to put a living thing to death against its will, as in a stray dog or a cat

expedition: a journey for a specific purpose such as for exploration, scientific research, or adventure

exploitation: the act of treating someone or something unfairly for one's own benefit; to overuse resources without asking

extinction: when a species dies out due to environmental forces or human intervention

gaff: a sharp metal spike or blade attached to a rooster's leg, often to make cockfights more dangerous or deadly

gillnet: a massive fishing net that hangs in the water like a wall

inhumane: unnecessarily cruel and causing pain or suffering to people or animals

mastitis: an infection in an udder that makes it swollen and painful

militia: a group of people organized for military purposes but who are not in the armed forces

neuter: surgically removing the reproductive organs of a male animal so it can't produce offspring

nonhuman primates: a group of mammals that includes monkeys, apes, gorillas, rhesus macaques, lemurs, and others

pet mill: a breeding facility where animals such as dogs and cats are bred as frequently as possible

physiology: the branch of biology that deals with the normal functions of living organisms and their body parts

purebred: an animal that is bred from parents of the same breed

regulate: to control or manage something by setting rules or guidelines. Regulation is the act of controlling or managing something through rules or laws.

safari: an overland journey to witness animals such as lions, elephants, and rhinoceroses in their natural habitats

spay: surgically removing the reproductive organs of a female animal so it can't produce offspring

traffic: to illegally trade or smuggle animals, often for profit

vaccine: a type of drug that protects the recipient from harmful or deadly diseases

vivisection: the process of operating on live animals for the purpose of scientific or medical research

wean: the process of gradually transitioning a young animal from its mother's milk to solid food

SOURCE NOTES

14 "We need to . . . of our scientists.": David Grimm, "EPA Scraps Plan to End Mammal Testing by 2035," ScienceInsider, January 12, https://www.science.org/content/article/epa-scraps-plan-end-mammal-testing-2035.

16 "the modern, industrialized . . . health and welfare.": "Animals in Agriculture & Aquaculture," Food Print, accessed August 5, 2024, https://foodprint.org/the-total-footprint-of-our-food-system/issues/animal-in-agriculture-aquaculture/.

19 "I act as . . . poor animal welfare.": Will Harris, *A Bold Return to Giving a Damn*, (New York: Viking, 2023), 123.

27 "In the face . . . this detrimental practice.": "136 NGOs Around the World Call for a Ban on Hunting Trophy Imports," Euro Group for Animals, July 6, 2022, https://www.eurogroupforanimals.org/news/136-ngos-around-world-call-ban-hunting-trophy-imports.

34 "Because they are . . . to do so.": Doris Lin, "Is Pet Ownership Ethical?" Treehugger, September 10, 2018, https://www.treehugger.com/arguments-for-and-against-keeping-pets-127752.

45 "Every day, countless . . . from such abuse.": "Bacon, Salinas Introduce Bipartisan Fight Inhumane Gambling and High-Risk Animal Trafficking Act," U.S. Congressman Don Bacon, April 20, 2023, https://bacon.house.gov/news/documentsingle.aspx?DocumentID=1220.

54 "Animals need our . . . and homeless animals.": "50 Ways Kids Can Help Animals," Humane Decisions, accessed August 5, 2024, https://humanedecisions.com/50-ways-kids-can-help-animals/.

SELECTED BIBLIOGRAPHY

Gallagher, Katherine. "Everything You Need to Know About Animal Testing for Cosmetics." Treehugger. June 22, 2022. https://www.treehugger.com/animal-testing-cosmetics-5202652.

Hall, Jani. "Poaching Animals, Explained." *National Geographic*. February 12, 2019. https://www.nationalgeographic.com/animals/article/poaching-animals.

Mooney, Taylor. "Congress Considers Crackdown on Trophy Hunting." CBS News. July 19, 2019. https://www.cbsnews.com/news/trophy-hunting-import-ban-cecil-act-hearing-in-congress/.

Whang, Oliver. "Cockfighting Is Illegal in the U.S. Why Does It Breed so Many Fighting Birds?" *New York Times Magazine*. January 18, 2023. https://www.nytimes.com/2023/01/18/magazine/cockfighting-rooster-breeding.html.

Zaveri, Mihir, Mariel Padilla, and Jaclyn Peiser. "E.P.A. Says It Will Drastically Reduce Animal Testing." *New York Times*. September 10, 2019. https://www.nytimes.com/2019/09/10/climate/epa-animal-testing.html.

FURTHER INFORMATION

Books

Barker, Justin, and Jane Goodall. *Bear Boy: The True Story of a Boy, Two Bears, and the Fight to Be Free*. Roseville, CA: Brutus & Ursula, LLC, 2021.
This memoir tells the true story of a young boy who fights to rescue two sibling black bears being kept in horrific conditions at a nearby zoo, gaining worldwide attention.

Eason, Sarah. *Helping Nature in Need: It's Time to Take Eco Action!* Minneapolis: Lerner, 2023.
This book teaches young people how to take care of Earth and the animals that live on it by exploring the lives and actions of some of the most eco-friendly organizations.

Kelaher, Catherine. *Saving Animals: A Future Activist's Guide*. Ashland, OR: Ashland Creek Press, 2021.
This book empowers young people to advocate and help animals through adopting veganism, becoming an activist, and volunteering.

Moon, Walt K. *Volunteering for Animal Welfare*. San Diego: BrightPoint Press, 2022.
This book explores ways that readers can get involved with animal welfare issues through volunteer work.

Nagle, Jeanne. *The Fight for Animal Rights*. New York: Rosen YA, 2019.
This book delves into the history of the animal rights movement and provides information about some of the public figures at the forefront of lobbying for animal welfare.

Newbery, Linda. *This Book Is Cruelty-Free: Animals and Us*. New York: Pavilion Books, 2021.
This book looks at the ways youth can change their everyday habits to be more cruelty-free, as well as educates on a variety of relevant animal and wildlife rights issues.

Websites

American Society for the Prevention of Cruelty to Animals (ASPCA)

https://www.aspca.org/

The first animal welfare organization in North America founded in 1866. This group works to rescue stray or abused animals and organize adoptions for those in need, fight against animal cruelty, provide disaster response, and advocate for the creation and enforcement of animal welfare laws in the United States.

Animal Justice

https://animaljustice.ca/

This group is Canada's only national animal law advocacy organization with a legal team that works to protect animals from neglect and abuse.

Humane League

https://thehumaneleague.org/article/animal-rights

This nonprofit organization aims to end the abuse of chickens, cows, pigs, and other animals raised for food by lobbying lawmakers and educating the public about hot-button topics such as factory farming and packaging labels.

Humane Society

https://www.humanesociety.org/resources/animal-cruelty-facts-and-stats

This website offers facts and statistics about animal abuse victims and the latest legislation involving animal welfare and protection.

INDEX

ABOUT THE AUTHOR

Alexis Burling has written dozens of articles and more than forty books for young readers on a variety of topics ranging from current events and biographies of famous people to nutrition and fitness to major milestones in history. She is also a professional book critic with reviews of adult and young adult books, author interviews, and other publishing industry-related articles published in the *New York Times*, the *Washington Post Book World*, *San Francisco Chronicle*, and more. Burling lives in Washington with her husband, rescue cats, and hundreds of books.

PHOTO ACKNOWLEDGMENTS

The images in this book are used with the permission of: © atm2003/Adobe Stock, p. 5; © INTERFOTO/Alamy Photo, p. 8; © recepaktas/Shutterstock Images, p. 10; © Elnur/Shutterstock Images, p. 12; © Imago/Alamy Photo, p. 13; © Ground Picture/Shutterstock Images, p. 14; © BearFotos/Shutterstock Images, p. 15; © Mark Agnor/Shutterstock Images, p. 18; © Janon Stock/Shutterstock Images, p. 20; © Rodica Vasiliev/Shutterstock Images, p. 21; © Jim Cumming/Shutterstock Images, p. 24; © Peter Marshall/Alamy Photo, p. 26; © Sean Herbert/AP Images, p. 27; © Danita Delimont/Alamy Photo, p. 29; © Paula Olson/AP Images, p. 31; © Xinhua/Alamy Photo, p. 33; © TheCats/Shutterstock Images, p. 35; © Tanya Dol/Shutterstock Images, p. 36; © KHANISTHA SRIDONCHAN/Shutterstock Images, p. 38; © Cheryl Ann Quigley/Shutterstock Images, p. 41; © Mary Swift/Shutterstock Images, p. 42; © Wassana Panapute/Shutterstock Images, p. 45; © dmitro2009/Shutterstock Images, p. 47; © Starz12/Shutterstock Images, p. 49; © SakSa/Shutterstock Images, p. 50; © Associated Press/AP Images, p. 51; © Mlle Sonyah/Shutterstock Images, p. 53; © Alberto/Adobe Stock, p. 55.

Cover Photo: © Galdric PS/Shutterstock Images

Design Elements: © Ezhevika/Shutterstock Images